Sungyeon Park

The Debate on South Korea's Industrial Policy Revisited

Sungyeon Park

The Debate on South Korea's Industrial Policy Revisited

LAP LAMBERT Academic Publishing

Impressum / Imprint

Bibliografische Information der Deutschen Nationalbibliothek: Die Deutsche Nationalbibliothek verzeichnet diese Publikation in der Deutschen Nationalbibliografie; detaillierte bibliografische Daten sind im Internet über http://dnb.d-nb.de abrufbar.
Alle in diesem Buch genannten Marken und Produktnamen unterliegen warenzeichen-, marken- oder patentrechtlichem Schutz bzw. sind Warenzeichen oder eingetragene Warenzeichen der jeweiligen Inhaber. Die Wiedergabe von Marken, Produktnamen, Gebrauchsnamen, Handelsnamen, Warenbezeichnungen u.s.w. in diesem Werk berechtigt auch ohne besondere Kennzeichnung nicht zu der Annahme, dass solche Namen im Sinne der Warenzeichen- und Markenschutzgesetzgebung als frei zu betrachten wären und daher von jedermann benutzt werden dürften.

Bibliographic information published by the Deutsche Nationalbibliothek: The Deutsche Nationalbibliothek lists this publication in the Deutsche Nationalbibliografie; detailed bibliographic data are available in the Internet at http://dnb.d-nb.de.
Any brand names and product names mentioned in this book are subject to trademark, brand or patent protection and are trademarks or registered trademarks of their respective holders. The use of brand names, product names, common names, trade names, product descriptions etc. even without a particular marking in this work is in no way to be construed to mean that such names may be regarded as unrestricted in respect of trademark and brand protection legislation and could thus be used by anyone.

Coverbild / Cover image: www.ingimage.com

Verlag / Publisher:
LAP LAMBERT Academic Publishing
ist ein Imprint der / is a trademark of
OmniScriptum GmbH & Co. KG
Heinrich-Böcking-Str. 6-8, 66121 Saarbrücken, Deutschland / Germany
Email: info@lap-publishing.com

Herstellung: siehe letzte Seite /
Printed at: see last page
ISBN: 978-3-659-75699-3

Zugl. / Approved by: Lund, Lund University, 2013

The Debate on South Korea's Industrial Policy Revisited

Sungyeon Park
SNGN.PRK@gmail.com

Abstract

Comprehending the East Asian Miracle has been a subject of heated major debate topic in development economics. And Korea was recognized as having one of the most pro-active state interventions in industrial policy and the debate on the performance of industrial policy has not been settled yet. This paper discusses the political economy of industrial policy over decades and the changes in conventional thinking in the World Bank on industrial policy. By reviewing the recent industrial policy debate on comparative advantage strategy in Korea by Justin Yifu Lin and Ha-Joon Chang this paper assesses the economic theory of comparative advantage and its work in Korean industrial policy, and it finds that Korea had defied from its comparative advantage too far during the process of industrialization despite of its success.

Key words

Industrial Policy, comparative Advantage, structural change, economic growth.

Table of Contents

List of tables and figures

Abbreviations

CAD Comparative Advantage Defying
CAF Comparative Advantage Following
FDI Foreign Direct Investment
GIFF Growth Identification and Facilitation Framework
HCI Heavy and Chemical Industry
HPE A High Performing East Asian Economies
IMF International Monetary Fund
NIE Newly Industrialized Economies
NSE New Structural Economics
TFP Total Factor Productivity
WB World Bank

Acknowledgements

In presenting this bachelor thesis, I would like to take this opportunity to express my gratitude to my supervisor, Martin Andersson who gave generously of his time, valuable comments and suggestions from his outstanding academic experiences. I would also like to thank all related teachers in economics and economic history department who have taught me in many different courses that have shaped intellectually and developed my understanding in studying development economics. Foremost, I would like to thank my parents – Kyungmi Nam and Songbong Park, through their hard works, commitments, and unconditional supports towards me, that made this work possible.

Any mistakes remain to the author's alone.

Lund, Sweden   Sungyeon Park
29th of May

1. Introduction

In my thesis research the focus is given to the role of state – industrial policy which is sensitive issue in economic policy, and it involves other contentious issues over legitimacy, morality, efficiency (Chang 1994:7), and how it had worked in South Korea (henceforth Korea)'s industrialization process if had it been correcting market failure, and reducing other external costs. Therefore, the political economy of industrial policy is a critical concept in my thesis research, - actually industrial policy itself is in a hard debate of defining its concept, but most commonly it means general industrial support policies; favoring promising industries; creating skilled workforces, fiscal and financial incentives for investment (Chang, 1994: 58), because there existed intensive debates on the role of the state/state intervention in industry, with suspicion from neo-classical economics. Nevertheless the recent economic rise of East Asia, where in strong industrial policy measures were implemented, renewed the debate, and academic interest on the applicability of industrial policy in other developing countries (Chang, 1994: 55).

It is debatable to what degree market failure has caused to demand increasing role of state along with the moral legitimacy and the political intention of state intervention to improve efficiency in an economy and to correct market failures (Chang, 1994:33). So understanding both institutional economics and political economy is indispensable for doing my research as my intention is to discuss institutional theory of state intervention, and political problem associated with industrial policy. Moreover, it generally tries to discuss market, state, and institutions in the context of industrialization process in Korea, but it specifically investigates whether the state's industrial policy was compatible *vis-à-vis* comparative advantage economic theory and it also looks on trade policy that whether government protection on the industry and trade area helped nurturing infant industries and industrial upgrading based on its comparative advantage or less-extend degree.

Although in the case of Korea's industrial policy had a substantial success, the state intervention theory is not unilateral to apply for solving efficiency, coordination, rent-seeking problem in countries with different conditions. By this reason thesis requires to have a construction of a sophisticated theory of state intervention, understanding economic theories/models to draw the benefits or the costs of state intervention in industrial policy.

Therefore, it is important to derive a verifiable implication of economic behavior of state intervention, to integrate, and interpret the concept of political economy of industrial policy with institutional economic approach to explain the proposed question based on empirical evidences and economic theories.

The thesis is organized into seven parts. The first part is methodology that presents research question and aim, and research method and strategies that used in this thesis. The second part discusses political economy of industrial policy which reviews briefly the previous industrial policy debates. The third part is recent Korean industrial policy debate which is the center of this thesis as the debate Korea's industrial policy is revisited, and examined for explaining its success in relation to the comparative advantage strategy. The fourth part discusses the World Bank's new thinking on industrial policy how recently it has changed its policy on the issue. The fifth part reviews comparative advantage theory – how the economic theory is still valid but what are the limitations of the theory in real world as well as how the theory is relevant to industrialization experience in Korea. The sixth part looks at the development experience of Korea how it overcame the difficulties of industrial upgrading beyond its latent comparative advantage and what were the benefits and costs of the industrial policy in the past decades. The last part is conclusion of the research paper.

2. Methodology
2.1 Research Question and Aim

Research question is originated from the historical evidence of the industrialization in Korea.

-What are the lessons from the past Korean industrial policy regarding comparative advantage theory and its strategy?

The aim of the research paper is to analysis critically on Korea's industrial policies from 1970s to 1980s, particularly focusing on the state's industrial policy to the promoted industries from 1970s, and by discussing the role of the state, market, and endogenous factor endowments as well as technological innovation for prompting economic structural change for economic growth and economic development to offer a deeper and wider understanding of Korea's development experience. And the main purpose of the research paper is to find on whether the country had pursued comparative advantage facilitating (CAF) or comparative advantage defying (CAD) strategy. This issue has been debated and rewritten among different traditions over many years. The research paper attempts to analyze and discuss critically the industrial success during the second half of 20 century in Korea, considering theoretical and empirical evidence from The New Structural Economics (NSE) based on a neoclassical approach and a counter argument by an approach from non-orthodox economists.

2.2. Research Method and Strategies

The research is conducted as a case study. Case study provides "a detailed and intensive analysis of a single case" while maintaining reliability, replicability, and validity of the case under consideration in order to answer designated research questions (Bryman, 2008: 66-69). And as a research method both qualitative and quantitative research are construed for the research, which respectively emphasizes a great deal of descriptive detail of historical evidence (Bryman, 2008:386), and quantification in the data collection and an analysis, and the testing the theory and hypothesis in a deductive approach in a relation to the research (Bryman, 2008:22).

This paper tries to test approach from The New Structural Economics which is based on neoclassical theory of comparative advantage. This gives the hypothesis 'Korea's industrial policy was successful because its policy was conformed to its comparative advantage for industrial upgrading', and the research tests it upon the historical evidence of industrial policies in Korea whether this hypothesis is confirmed or rejected through collected data and finding.

The process of deduction approach is followed such ways: Theory-Hypothesis-Data collection-Findings-Hypothesis confirmed or rejected-Revision of Theory (Bryman, 2008:10).

2.2-1 Secondary Analysis of Data

Many of the techniques, questionnaire, structured interview, structured observation and content analysis used in research methods can be extremely time-consuming and expensive to conduct. In most of cases undergraduate students doing research, besides their limited capability as an amateur, have neither time nor the financial resources to conduct very extensive research. And we know already, large amounts of quantitative data are collected by other researchers, governments departments and various institutions in the course of their interests (Bryman, 2008: 295) and it is available publicly.

As the research aim and the question of this paper shows, the research paper is designed for an essay based on economic theories, and historical evidence. Most of all, there are already vast amounts of several published academic journals, and books by distinguished researchers. So, the research paper uses the strategy of re-interpretation of secondary data to produce a better research outcome which is largely contributed by data collection and analysis but the limitations to complexity and control of data quality (Bryman, 2008:300).

Fortunately, the country, Korea case study has already good statistical, other existing data to analysis in the particular period of industrial policies practiced by the state. And this provided good quality of resources.

One of several reasons why secondary data should be taken, but most importantly, is that it allowed me to spend more time on the analysis and interpretation of the data, and economic models, and theories I collected. (Bryman, 2008:296). And reanalysis of secondary data may offer new interpretations, (Bryman, 2008:299) as discussed in following chapter there is still debate among different school of thoughts on explaining industrial success in Korea by their interpretations of economic models, theories, historical, and quantitative evidence whether did the state's industrial policies followed fully comparative advantage facilitating or defying strategy.

2.2-2 Literature Review

This is also about reviewing relevant literatures, which are already known about my area of interest, and exploring relevant literatures will help me to understand works of others, developing an analytic framework and an argument about the significance of my research. It is important to be clear that, this process is not just a matter of reproducing the theories and opinions of other scholars, but to interpret it in a systematic review, which is often seen as supplement to evidence based approaches, generating unbiased and comprehensive accounts of the literature (Bryman, 2008:85). And possibly using theoretical ideas to support a particular viewpoint or argument (Bryman, 2008:81), where in this case, I look upon the industrialization period in Korea.

2.2-3 Shortcomings

The topic is quite broad even for a country case study level and complex as it is related to many other areas such as trade policy, foreign direct investment (FDI), labor market for the deeper understanding of industrial policy. However, by the limitation of resources, time, and other restrictions these issues would not be discussed much here but for the simplicity the paper tries to make a general discussion of industrial policy in Korea, as well as an assessment of the comparative advantage theory and strategy in 1970s, and the costs and benefits of the policy.

3. Political Economy of Industrial Policy

Neo-liberalism has been the dominant economic doctrine of the last three decades, as its name implies which tradition goes back to the founder of economics, Adam Smith. He famously rejected the conventional idea of his day - government intervention, planning, and public ownership in the economy, arguing it would generally harmful to the economy. Instead, he advocated the virtue of free market, as referring famously 'invisible hand', and self-interested people in his book the wealth of nations would take care of the market price, output, and profit (Yoo, 1990; Buchholz, 2007:30).

His idea of free trade based on absolute advantage of one country was advanced by Ricardo, who claimed that countries should specialize in a good that have the least opportunity cost, which is their comparative advantage (Buchholz, 2007:74). Both Smith and Ricardo blasted protectionist idea that government subsidizes merchants through quota or tariff against foreign competition but consumers would have to take a burden of higher price. Neither, 'Infant industry' argument that suggests a temporary protection in an early stage of economic development until they become mature and competitive in an international market is cogently accepted by them (Buchholz, 2007:38).

Nevertheless, in economic history when look at closer the history of capitalism it tells a different story. At least, according to the most prominent non-orthodox economist Chang Ha-Joon (2002), he debunks neo-liberal arguments in his book 'Kicking away the ladder' that the idea of infant industry in historical perspective as a development strategy to promote their national industries was embraced virtually numerous times by almost the early industrialized countries, from Great Britain to Western Europe and the

United States to Japan, and Newly Industrialized Economies (NIE) such as Korea.

Although the *laissez-faire* approach of free trade, market, industrial - let's say 'liberal' economic policy was dominant intellectual framework in the last centuries, and for sure it provided a root of economic growth with many good insights on the process of economic development, it underestimated in many points such as socio-economic, political change, technological change, the role state, and institutions ina n economy.

In the modern economic history industrial debate has been evolved and it has been one of the most contentious topics in development economics. Until recently in the mainstream economics industrial policy or known as 'picking the winners' by the state has been seen as a wrong policy, in other words, seen as an anathema by free market economists (Chang, 1994).

The idea of industrial policy was discredited in the past 1950s and 1960s when countries in Latin America and Africa adopted numerous industrial policies involving strong state interventions, which turned out badly in economic performance of these countries. And mainstream economic policies have gone towards more liberalization of an economy in developing countries following 'Washington Consensus' and international financial institutions - the World Bank and International Monetary Fund (IMF).

However, so called 'East Asian Miracle', over three decades of impressive economic growth and development experiences of East Asian economies such as (including Japan early), Singapore, Hong Kong, Taiwan, and Korea, reinvigorated industrial policy debate as these economies (less relevant to Singapore, and Hong Kong) implemented industrial policy by the state at some stages of that high economic growth period (Lee, 2011).

In early decades mainstream (neoclassical) economists (still) did not pay attention to the industrial policy and thus the role of state for a major contribution of their high economic growth achievements. Rather they explained their successes attributing mainly to free trade, liberalization, more broadly market friendly approach-driven mechanism (Krueger, 1974). This view has been challenged by other heterodox economists (Johnson, 1982; Amsden, 1989; Wade, 1990; Chang, 1994) who criticized market failure, and with developmental state approach credited the state's industrial policy for their high economic growth experience. If there has been recognition of industrial policy implementation in 'high performing East Asian economies' (HPEA) in recent decades, the debate on results of it has been divided by some who argue that the effect of it was only marginal on their economic growth performances (World Bank, 1993; Noland & Pack, 2003; Pack & Saggi, 2006). And the others who insisted that industrial policy had some beneficial effects on industrialization (Rodrik, 1995, 1996, 2008; Stiglitz, 1996; Hausmann & Rodrik, 2003).

11

Recently, Lin and Monga (2010), and a book 'New Structural Economics (NSE)' published by Lin (2011), former chief economist of the World Bank put forwards the debate on the new direction if not back to the starting point or backward. The major step forward from the neoclassical economist is to acknowledge the importance of the role of state in industrial upgrading. He argues that the main purpose of the state is to identify its comparative advantage and facilitate economic activities by helping firms/enterprises to explore its comparative advantage. But, still the advanced neoclassical approach remains constrained by sticking to comparative advantage theory, implicitly arguing for free market and free trade ideology in policy. Which has drawn new criticisms from other (including heterodox) economists (Singh, 2011).

So far, the debate on the performances of industrial policy in HPEA has not been settled in a firm agreement and assessment of economic growth performance of industrial policy has remained a major research area in development economics (Krugman & Obsfeld, 2006: 255).

4. Recent Korean Industrial Policy Debate

This is a starting point of my discussion in the research paper, taking Korea as a case study, to analysis the period of industrialization, and to find an explanation for the industrial success as introduced approach from The New Structural Economics (NSE) by Justin Yifu Lin and a following counter argument from non-orthodox economists such as Ha-Joon Chang. Ideas drawn from their main arguments, and data I brought I suggest a third option, which can be a compromise between a slight different point of two economists.

In a simple way industrial development strategy can be divided into two exclusive groups, the Comparative Advantage Defying (CAD) strategy and the Comparative Advantage Following (CAF) strategy. The former strategy attempts to encourage firms to enter industries that are not within their current comparative advantages, and existing technology. On the other hand, the latter strategy leads firms to conform to their existing comparative advantages (Lin, 2011:295).

Two prominent economists, Justin Yifu Lin and Ha-Joon Chang who came from different theoretical traditions made a short debate in this issue. Although both economists agreed on the importance of industrial upgrading and the role of the state in the process against market failure, and coordination failure in different input markets, they differed in how far a country should defy from the comparative advantage.

Ha-Joon believes comparative advantage is important but as just base line, that country should defy from its comparative advantage in order to upgrade its industry. He takes historical examples from early industrialization in Western Europe to Japan, and Korea, all of them had used protectionist industrial measures as it referred to 'infant industry protection' (Chang, 2002; 2004). He argues the theory of neoclassical comparative advantage approaches from Justin ignores limited factor mobility, and the lack of technological capability which is common in many developing countries, and underestimates costs of trade liberalization and the need for good distribution mechanism. Therefore, a certain length and strength of wished specific industrial sector protection is required, giving examples of Toyota, Nokia, and Pohang Steel companies (Lin and Chang, 2009).

However, Justin argues that, over the past 40 years, Korea has managed to achieve the remarkable economic success, as it proved the GDP per capita grew rapidly over 20 years (Figure 1) and it gained successful recognition internationally in automobiles, electronics, semiconductors, and shipbuilding industries (Lin and Chang, 2009; Lin, 2011: 127).

Figure 1. Korea's GDP per Capita

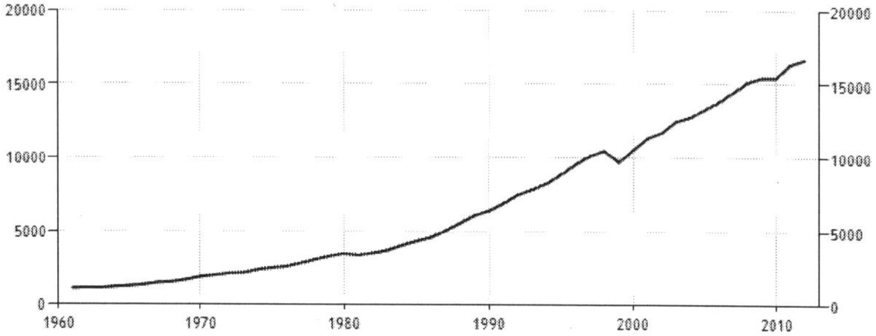

GDP Per Capita in US Dollars at Constant Prices Since 2000

Source: World Bank

He gives some reasons why Korea had succeeded a rapid industrialization in the past decades. He argues as other many developing countries Korea was very poor after World War II and in 1950s the level of industrialization, GDP per capita was very low, capital and foreign exchange reserves were limited. Although at initial stages it adopted an import substitution CAD strategy to develop heavy industries in a short period, however converted later to CAF strategy based on the outward export-led, labor intensive industrialization using its latent comparative advantage based on current factor endowments at full extent(Lin, 2011:308).

Thus, Korea adopted a realistic approach to the industrial upgrading, for which the country adjusted its industrial policy strategy to entering specific industries that had a consistency with its current and/or evolving comparative advantage, *ceteris paribus,* based on factor endowment which determines the relative factor prices therefore, reflecting the optimal industrial structure of the country (Ju et al., 2009).

It gradually moved ladder of industrial structure from labor intensive to more capital, technology intensive one because of an increasing abundance of capital through exports and an increase of wage rates (Lin, 2011:308). Otherwise, even the targeted industries with the advantage of backwardness for industrial upgrading and diversification are unlikely to succeed because of the costly 'trial and error' exercise of discovery in its economy's comparative advantage (Hausmann and Rodrik, 2003).

He backs his argument with historical evidences, which are influenced and, interpreted from his advanced neo-classical approach in New Structural Economics. So, in 1960s Korea developed and exported labor-intensive products such as garments, wigs, plywoods. Meanwhile, Korea built up a large amount of capital reserves from exports revenue, and its endowment structure changed constantly, which drove fast its industrial structure into more capital intensive, and high-tech/skills based industries such as automotive, chemical, shipbuilding with great help of state's industrial policy (Lin and Chang,2009; Lin, 2011:77).

He emphasizes although industrial structural transformation was rapid, and upgrading, at the initial stage still domestic manufactures focused mostly on assembly of imported parts, which was demanded labor-intensive manufacturing process, which was aligned with its comparative advantage. For example, electronics industry mainly worked for producing household products like TVs, washing machines, prior to moving on the production of memory chips, the least technologically complex segment of information technology industry (Lin and Chang, 2009; Lin, 2011:77). He reflects the industrial upgrading, and the rapid technological ascent process was stimulated by a synergistic relation between the dynamic growth, and rapid accumulation of physical and human capital.

In the industrialization process the role of the Korean state as "a facilitating state" was crucial. It clearly recognized the successful industrial upgrading depended on performance of firms that are influenced by world prices for both input and out prices. Therefore, the state operated its industrial policy to provide intermediate inputs at world price for manufacturers through incentive schemes and export-processing zones, and it managed the protected sectors kept to market discipline, and refrained large-scale deviation from the latent comparative advantage

(Lin and Chang, 2009; Lin, 2011:128). His argument implies that the rate of growth could have been faster if industrial sectors remained consistent with its comparative advantage without the protectionist measures implemented by the state.

He goes further by saying, if a country follows Ha-Joon's recommendation for using trade policy based on the basic idea of dynamic comparative advantage and infant-industry protection, as a tool for industrial upgrading, simply say attempting to a big leap without going through step by step in the conjunction with evolving its comparative advantage, the learning costs would be much higher because the protected industries would be viable just for a few decades or less. Losses made by these protected infant industries would have to be covered by profit making industries which are in current comparative advantage (Lin and Chang, 2009; Lin, 2011:129). This resource allocation would reduce the surpluses of the latter industries. Moreover it would cause slow-down of capital accumulation and the upgrading of endowment structure and comparative advantage (Baldwin, 1969; Saure, 2007). Besides that, excessive and exaggerated infant industry protection would risk to produce rent seeking behavior of the protected industries, lowering the quality of institutions and governance (Lin and Chang, 2009).

Differentiate with the old structural economics that advocated protection and subsidies to protect existing industries and to build new industries that are not compatible with current comparative advantage, he suggests in New Structural Economics (NSE), the dual-track, gradual approach for government in transition economies to move towards gradual trade liberalization, with temporary protection or subsidies to old industries to re-allocate their resources into a system of market-based prices under favorable conditions where they have a comparative advantage avoiding further unnecessary and costly economic and social disruption (Lin, 2011:78).

In which industry restructuring process could be described as a "flying-geese" pattern of economic development, relocating specific capital or less competitive old existing industry in the form of foreign direct investment to other countries (Akamatsu, 1962; Suehiro,2008; ch 2, 6 ,13)

He believes that there is no doubt that active industrial and trade policies in Korea hindered growth substantially during the industrialization take-off. The country had used protectionist measures in certain sectors against foreign competitions, even some cases the state took aggressive move to capital intensive industries for industrial upgrading. Despite of that, Justin explains behind the industrialization success of Korea, it was largely because the country followed its comparative advantage although he acknowledges the fact Korea defied its comparative advantage, but not far as it was argued by Ha-Joon (Lin and Chang, 2009).

In summary, their differences lie in defining 'far' - a degree of deviation from the comparative advantage that a country may pursue, and interpretation of the trade model, historical evidence, and how to promote technological learning cost-effectively (Lin and Chang, 2009). Based upon these differences this paper assesses Korean industrial policy with comparative advantage theory and its strategy used in the next pages.

5. The World Bank's new Thinking on Industrial Policy

First of all, Justin Lin, who was the former chief economist at the World Bank and introduced New Structural Economics (NSE), acknowledged the proactive industrial policy and the decisive role of the state in economic development, particularly referencing the East Asian Economies. Therefore, these changes in attitudes on industrial policy led by the state are a quite major step forward by the World Bank. The institution's traditionally theoretical underpinnings lighted by the history of economic thought and theory but it has been comprehensively modified from the anti-state, anti-traditional industrial policy thinking which pervaded during much of the 1990s and 2000s (Singh, 2011).

'A half-century later, it remains true that there are few if any examples of governments that have succeeded with a purely laissez-faire approach that does not try to come to grips with market failures, and far more examples of rapid growth in countries whose governments have led effectively. Therefore, it is incumbent upon policy-makers and researchers to identify the most effective ways of promoting the productivity growth and change in industrial structure necessary for development.'

'Neither of us questions the importance of a major state role in promoting economic development. Perhaps this is because in the countries we know most intimately _ China and South Korea _ a crucial ingredient in growth was a capable and largely developmentally oriented state. The issue is identifying the key role played by the state in those countries and other rapid developers (Lin and Chang, 2009).'

New Structural Economics (NSE) is a new step forward from the past three decades of neo-classical thinking, in which a role of state is enhanced. The major issue for the state is of identifying key industries in an economy. Lin argues that state should act like a 'facilitating' state by identifying a country's existing comparative advantage and guiding direction (coordination) of productive activities for enterprises and firms should be a main purpose of pursuing the state's industrial policy because "trial and error process" is likely to be long and costly (Lin and Chang, 2009).

He reasons that state intervention is undertaken with assumption of severe market failures, for instance resolving negative externalities, incomplete information with regard to products and process coordination of economic agents in market that need to be corrected by artificial force, preferably by the state. And to reach optimal industrial structure a country should follow endogenous process of upgrading, which requires first to recognize its factor endowment in terms of abundance of labor and skills, capital, and natural resources by the state, and to make sure that a country is integrated with the world economy, and the economic growth led by the exports is based on its comparative advantage by encouraging free trade and capital movement. This would make a country competitive domestically and internationally. Otherwise any efforts to defying its comparative advantage would fail because it would be too costly for private side or state (Singh 2011).

However, its encouragement of industrial policy compatible with its latent comparative advantage based on factor endowments, which implicitly advocate for the unconditional openness to world economy, and it is going back to the first principle of classical economic thought as well as economic theory and economic history (Singh, 2011), and this argument seems not to fit well with development experience, at least in case of Korea from the historical perspective.

6. Reviewing Comparative Advantage Theory

The theory of comparative advantage is few of founding classical economic thoughts that are commonly accepted in economics. The beauty of this theory is how a country with no absolute international cost advantage would have a chance to increase its current consumption bundle to be benefited from the international trade by specializing in any industry that has low opportunity costs than others, based on its current factor endowments (Chang and Lin, 2009; Lin,2011, 121).

However, the flaw of HOS theory is well- known, especially in the Heckscher-Ohlin-Samuelson version Justin uses is the stringent assumption of perfect factor mobility (within each country). The theory assumes that factor mobility in any sectors caused by external effects of trade pattern would be reallocated in another sector without great losses. For instance resources in less competitive sector would be reallocated resource into the same or higher levels of productivity sectors, which also have higher returns. In the end no one loses from the process (Lin and Chang, 2009; Lin, 2011:122).

Perhaps to study in short term resource allocation efficiency (if a country interested in knowing whether given resources are exploited in a maximum efficiency) this theory would be acceptable but for the medium-term adjustment and long term economic development this theory would be problematic. Because first when one looks at medium-term adjustment, in reality the factors of production is fixed in their physical qualities, so for instance bankrupted steel industry cannot be re-moulded into electronics industries unless workers are retrained at best, but still many will remain unemployed or end up working in low-skilled jobs. In other words even in the country liberalize its trade, economy fully the owners of low or no mobility of factors of production are going to lose from competition, unless there is a compensation provided by the state or other means. Which is non-existent or weak in most of developing countries (Chang and Lin, 2009; Lin, 2011:122). An example of this is shown in next pages arguing there were no great positive intersectoral externalities between labor intensive and capital intensive industries in Korea.

In the long-term economic development, the HOS theory about technology can be misleading in reality, by assuming there is only one best technology for producing a specific good, and most of all most of countries (regardless of developing or developed countries) have the same capability to use that technology. This assumption clearly undermines the different capabilities to develop and use technologies, which is known as "technological capabilities", as the rich/developed countries have that capabilities to use, and develop technologies fully, on the other hand less developed and developing countries have not (Chang and Lin, 2009; 2011: 123).

Moreover, conventionally defined Standard Heckscher-Ohlin theory was formulated in an earlier time than recent globalization era which allows the kinds of freely mobile capital flows, apart from agriculture, where in the factor endowment does not provide the basis of production and specialization patterns (Stiglitz, 2011). Rather, the theory is a static to ignore the existing forward linkages between present choices and future production possibilities (Succar, 1987).

Simply, countries do not need to constrain their potential economic growth by the endowments any longer. But the most important elements of factor endowment should be "knowledge" and "entrepreneurship". Indeed, knowledge is not the same as other physical factors that contribute to total productivity function. Sharing knowledge does not discount others' utility or make others worse off. Knowledge is associated with externalities - spillover effects. For that reason, it is compelling to argue that the improvements and producing in knowledge as a primary source for growth in developing countries, not just a gap in resource with developed countries (Stiglitz, 2011) as well as the advances in technology, which have been recognized that the major source of increases in per capita income (Solow, 1957) although there is an argument that growth rate of total factor productivity in the East Asian economies was low at the initial stage of a rapid economic growth period (World Bank, 1993: Chapter 6 and Pack, 2000). But when these economies gradually moved from the labor intensive to capital intensive industries so did income per capita and TFP also increased dramatically as well.

Certainly, comparative advantage theory does offer a profound insight that the country pays more the costs by protecting its infant industries in order to gain technology capabilities in new industries, thus it should be avoided - deviating too much from one's comparative advantage. However, this does not denote a country should conform to its comparative advantage, it was simply not easy if not impossible for a 'extreme backward country' like Korea to develop its capabilities for moving into new advanced industries without defying its comparative advantage, and eventually entering the industries before it attains optimal factor endowments that reflect an industrial structure (Lin and Chang, 2009; Lin, 2011:124).

Deciding when to enter a new industry by using cost-benefit analysis – (it weighs the costs of technological upgrading against expected future returns using comparative advantage) as the measuring rod is logical, but the problem of uncertainty arises how to predict the acquisition of necessary technological capabilities and expected future benefit (returns) unless a country actually enters the industry and develop it (Chang in Lin, 2011:124). And it may be argued that usually states in developing countries had no capability to identify its comparative advantage (Pack and Saggi, 2006).

Therefore, in order to catch up with technologically advanced developed countries in terms of technological gap/capabilities, it may be said that a country has to set up and protect specific industries with less comparative advantage but specific industries a country wishes to develop. However, factor accumulation is not an abstract process that happens spontaneously, a country cannot remain to see its physical and human capital to accumulate enough to enter into a more advanced industry.

Unfortunately, even if a country has the favorable capital-labor ratio for the automobile industry it cannot enter the industry if the accumulated capital is formed as textile machines. In the same way, even if a country accumulated sufficient human capital to establish the automobile industry still it cannot make cars if all of them are trained as engineers and workers for the textile industry (Lin and Chang, 2009; Lin, 2011:123).

Improving technological capabilities requires accumulation of concrete production experiences, which in the form of 'collective knowledge' embodied in. This is potentially very lengthy learning process, which cannot be acquired overnight, so even if a country has a right capital, labor, and machines, an international competitiveness would not be achieved (Lin and Chang, 2009; Lin, 2011:124).

Industrial sector has a large spillover effect and encouraging investment in specific industrial sectors by learning by doing was crucial in Korea, at the center of creating a learning society

22

(Greenwald and Stiglitz, 2006). Neoclassical economic theory emphasizes a short run static efficiency, but had Korea followed what market forces entail it to produce rice; agricultural products, it might have been today one of the most efficient rice producers but it would not have embarked on its quite successful industrialization path (Stiglitz, 2011).

A form of structural change, shifting the unskilled rural labor force to unskilled labor-intensive industries may not occur spontaneously. By the reason, identification and facilitation of growth of existing and potential industries, and prioritization of limited resource allocation by government industrial policy are crucial for successful growth strategy and industrialization. In 1980 although 34 percent of Korea's labor force was in agriculture sector, the country already entered not only consumer electronics, but also shipbuilding, automobile, memory chip considered to be capital intensive, high tech industries at the time (Lin, 2011:68).

Thus, Korea's 'ladder' of international division of labor has often carried out in rapid step, and the moves into industries like steel and shipbuilding were considered as big leaps, without virtually no intermediate steps. (Lin and Chang, 2009; Lin, 2011:132) This point is confirmed in intersectoral externalities between weaving in light industries and other industries in heavy industries, there were no significant beneficial effects from the former sector to the latter (Amsden, 1989). And this could explain excessive learning costs of promoted industries in Korea.

As one of measures to assess its comparative advantage at the period, GDP per capita in current dollar term gives a dramatic example how Korea was immature to enter the heavy and chemical industries in comparison to the U.S standards. For example POSCO (Pohang Iron and Steel Company), the former state owned steel mill company was established in 1968 and it started its production in 1972. In the same year the state decided ambitiously to enter Heavy and Chemical Industrialization Program, which consisted of shipbuilding, automobiles, machinery, and many other high tech, skilled, and capital intensive industries. At the time its GDP per capita was a mere 5.5% that of the U.S. ($322 VS. $5,838)[1]. And electronic industry

---

[1] All the current dollar income figures are from
http://www.nationmaster.com/red/graph/eco_gdp_percapeconomy-gdp-per-capita, which draws on the World Bank and the CIA data

the one of nation's key industries– semiconductors and computers were promoted by the state from 1976 for almost two decades, ($824 VS. $8,297) [World Bank, 1978] and in late 1983, Samsung decided to develop semiconductors sector, when Korea's income was only 14% that of the U.S ($2,118 vs. $ 15, 008), these industries were not hardly fell within its comparative advantage either.

If Justin's explanation is correct that Korea's industrial policy was consistent with its comparative advantage, then at the time country's income per capita, less than 6% that of U.S. would be testifying its theory of comparative advantage? Certainly this claim would not hold.

But, Justin defends his argument by explaining that the deviation from its comparative advantage was not greater than what actually Ha-Joon sees because Korea's industrial policy was modeled on Japan, not the U.S. as the above per capita income differences show. As Korea's development model Japan was relatively less developed, having lower-income than U.S. When the Korean state tried to facilitate industrial upgrading (e.g., automobile industry development) in 1960s and 1970s, per capita income was about 35 % that of Japan (Lin, 2011:156).

This argument could be close to what he suggested in New Structural Economics (NSE) with its Growth Identification and Facilitation Framework (GIFF) model, in where first step of six steps is to follow:

'Governments should select dynamically growing countries with a similar endowment structure and with about 100% higher per capita income than their own average. They must then identify tradable industries that have grown well in those countries for the previous 20 years (Lin, 2011:181).'

But even following his GIFF model Korea should have waited until the income reach about 50% that of Japan. Otherwise, a long deviation from its comparative advantage in the promoted industries, through 'big-push' attempts which required the state's coordination, the demand spillovers to other industries (Murphy, Shleifer, and Vishny, 1989a, 1989b) was costly.

However, Justin insists that industrial upgrading is a continuous process, in which the state needs to help solve externality and coordination problems, and help firms exploit its existing, shifting comparative advantages and its endowment structure. And the state owned POSCO, steel company was investment, largely built on the success of labor-intensive industries of garments, plywoods, wigs, footwear and others. From these industries Korea accumulated capital and the increased capital intensity of factor endowment structure and shifting a few firms into more capital intensive industries was necessary (Lin, 2011:135).

Furthermore, he argues that Korea were able to succeed in the steel industry because capital intensive industries such as steel and shipbuilding no longer held leading edge position in the global technological frontier, as these industries traced from centuries of long history and their technologies have become mature, thus capital intensities were much lower than the new emergent industries in global industrial spectrum and easy to mobilize a large amount of capital by the state's support (ibid).

In contrast with his argument, the fourth and fifth panel of the table 1 shows that a Korean steel company, POSCO has been extremely capital intensive, as it has utilized more capital than competitors to produce each unit of output, as seen that it has increased capital intensity over time, to surpass its competitors from Japan and U.S., and this was partly attributed to its extraordinary success in terms of labor productivity and profitability (Lieberman and Kang 2008).

Table 1. Comparison of POSCO with Nippon Steel (Japanese) and USX (U.S.) Steel Companies from 1973 to 2003

	1973	1983	1993	2003	Annual Growth Rate 1973–2003
1. Total sales (tons shipped ×1,000)					
POSCO	534	7,706	21,183	28,202	14.1%
Nippon Steel	31,400	26,700	25,320	29,902	−0.2%
USX	26,100	NA	9,969	14,399	−2.0%
2. Operating profit/sales					
POSCO	20%	16%	15%	21%	
Nippon Steel	10%	3%	4%	5%	
USX	12%	NA	−3%	−8%	
3. Labor productivity (a) (Value-added per worker hour)					
POSCO	1,664	6,431	13,010	21,586	8.9%
Nippon Steel	4,492	5,371	9,245	17,130	4.6%
USX	5,209	NA	5,565	5,640	0.3%
4. Fixed capital per employee (b)					
POSCO	19.2	73.0	94.6	130.7	6.6%
Nippon Steel	27.8	33.0	39.5	67.4	3.0%
USX	8.9	NA	28.0	25.0	3.5%
5. Fixed capital per ton shipped (c)					
POSCO	142.9	137.2	101.1	89.8	−1.5%
Nippon Steel	71.2	80.1	56.6	37.1	−2.1%
USX	63.3	NA	60.5	40.3	−1.5%
6. Multifactor productivity (d)					
POSCO	51.6	62.6	107.1	133.5	3.2%
Nippon Steel	78.6	82.6	131.6	182.4	2.8%
USX	126.9	NA	101.8	103.9	−0.7%

(a) 1980 yen per hour.

(b) Millions of 1980 yen

(c) Thousands of 1980 yen.

(d) Nippon Steel = 100 in 1980.

Source: Lieberman and Kang (2008)

When the state decided to promote an integrated iron and steel making facility the country lacked the technical skills and economic resources necessary to produce steel efficiently, as a learner rather than innovator at the initial stage, creating competitive advantage in steel industry was a turning point in Korean industrial history (Amsden, 1989:292)because unlike textiles industry –which tended to involve capital widening capacity expansion, the steel industry tended to involve large simultaneous capital deepening process – in which indivisible embodying of new technology and skill and an increasing capital/labor ratio it required to create value in dynamic learning (Hawtrey, 1937), and it has to raise higher productivity not just lower prices and wages to compete against the industrial leaders like Japan and U.S. (Amsden, 1989:292).

It may be argued that besides the ideas of comparative advantage, self-discovery, and the facilitating state, to move beyond 'middle-income trap', more considerable strategic policy is required to take risk jumping into non-mature, higher value-added (have less comparative advantage) industries that it wishes to develop. This is because there are the missing links (linkages) in the domestic value chain, which cannot automatically move up the ladder of industrial sector, therefore it requires the industrial policy by the state to make concerted efforts to target industries and develop them under protection (Lim, 2011).

According to Amsden (1989) economic side of externality appears that there had been a significantly positive intersectoral externalities between two phases in Korea, where - foreign exchange revenue, employment generated by light manufactured exports sector helped develop more skill and capital intensive manufacturing sectors.

On the contrary, techno-managerial externalities had no major effects from light manufactures in general to more complex industrial activities in Korea (Amsden, 1989:155) except electronics and the automobile industry in which sector the development of new products was based on the past accumulated technological capabilities within. Cross-industry externality came mostly from the interactions of each individual industries within the promoted and non-promoted industries respectively rather than promoted and non-promoted industries (Pack, 2000).

For these reasons that idea of comparative advantage (relative prices), specialization enhances growth does not bear the weight of facts in structural transformation in the last industrialization, but in reality an intermediate role of the state to initiate progress of structural transformation through in the form of subsidies and other protective measures was crucial in industrial upgrading, which permitted a limited period of import substitution to diversify of export products in order to catch up (Amsden, 1989:155).

7. Creation of Dynamic Comparative Advantage and its Costs and Benefits of industrial policy in Korea

Although it is true that Korea developed labor intensive light industries by exploiting its latent comparative advantage facilitating strategy in the 1960s as Justin suggested, it didn't wait until its skills, and income rose enough to enter into high-value added capital intensive industries (Lim, 2011).

It is important to remind that after World War II the U.S. was a clear technological leader in most industries, and even though first Asian modernizer, Japan was still behind of the U.S, but ahead of Korea. Therefore, it is plausible to designate it as an "extremely backward" country compared to those two countries, and it gives a reason why the country had to adopt the Gerschenkronian substituting strategies - focusing on building internationally competitive local industries (Shin and Chang, 2003:11).

Thus, true aim of industrial policy designed by the state was acquiring comparative advantage in the high tech industries to catch up with advanced (neighbor) countries like Japan, not in smokestack or lower end of activities of higher technology industries (Lee, 2011).

After benchmarking the development model of Japan, which had similar natural endowments for the previous decades Korea recognized its potential comparative advantage in advanced capital intensive industries beyond assembly lines and despite of the considerable risks of failure, high costs, and unprecedented infant industry protection time, industrial policy was initiated to support the plan mostly through five-year development plan (Lim, 2011).

Therefore, to catch up with early industrialized countries the state pursued industrial policy with utmost vigor in the name of 'heavy and chemical industry (HCI) policy in 1970s (Yoo, 1990) and later 'high-tech' industries as crucial steps for an independent national economy building. It diversified its exports from less to more skill - and capital intensive industries in a non-linear way. And it implies that the ladder of upgrading comparative advantage stage was a matter of creating competitiveness (Amsden, 1989:144).

HC industries were 'new' industries, implying that these industries had no comparative advantages at all, thus it was required to have a large-scale capital mobilization and a long gestation period of investment it eventually paid off without knowing the end. And the success of those promoted HC industries was determined by *chaebols* structure, with centralized control and a high degree of internal diversification (Shin and Chang, 2003:29). Strategically, the state sought to indigenize intermediate inputs of imported technologies, increase supply of skilled labor forces (human capital development) - state-led, part of industrial policy for nurturing skilled engineers, technicians to fill in sophisticated industries was at this time, and the construction of optimal scale plants aiming for international market (Amsden, 1989; Lim, 2011).

Empirical results confirm this argument that Korea has went through a rapid structural transformation from the 1970s (Figure2), and the growth rates of output and composition of value-added between the promoted and non-promoted industries (table 2.) have changed as it shows that promoted (infant) industries have grown faster and taken over non-promoted industries, eventually they became matured showing that the improved international competitiveness of these promoted industries. Indeed, industrial policy by the state had succeeded in 'picking the winners' (Lee, 2011) but rather at the high costs.

Figure 2. Structural Change in Korea (1963-2009)

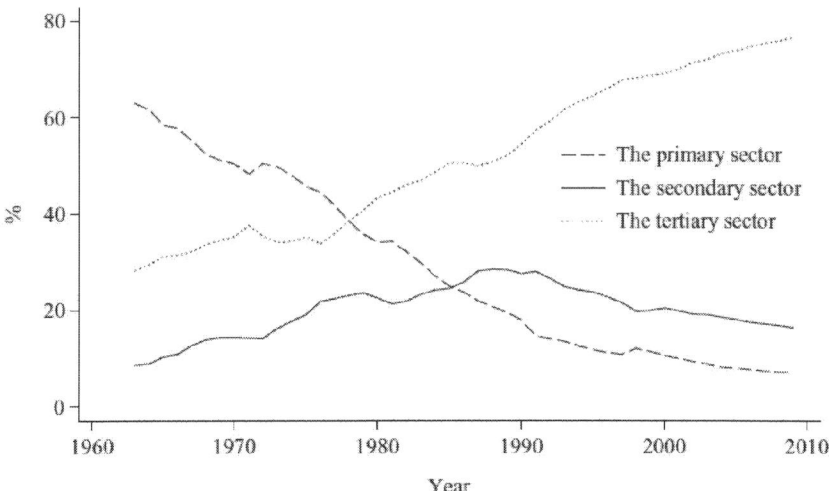

Source: Mao and Yao (2012)

Source: Korean Statistical Information Service, Statistics Korea.
Notes: Employment shares are presented. The primary sector includes agriculture, forestry and fishing. The secondary sector is a combination of mining and manufacturing. The tertiary sector contains s.o.c and other services, such as electricity and gas, construction, wholesale, retail, restaurant, hotels, transportation, storage, communication, finance, insurance, real estate, business ,government and others

It is crucial that understanding Korea's industrialization- with the role of Korean state and firms, as it was led by the state-owned enterprises and family-based groups (*Chaebol*) with successive performance records to minimize time, costs, and to exploit scale economies in building capital intensive industries (Lim, 2011). The Korean state undertook to set strategic industries, by providing subsidies, bank financing and protections to firms; the *chaebol* to build new industries, and this pattern of central economic system can be drawn as the state-banks-*chaebol*. So, regulated monopoly or oligopoly by *chaebol* in these industries were allowed until the scale of domestic demand reaches enough to support effective competition (Shin and Chang, 2003:13). The state adopted industrial policy and guided the commercial banks to provide cheap credits to targeted promoted industries (Shin and Chang, 2003:32). In fact, the mutual relationship between the state, banks, and firms are a lot more complex than described here.

Table 2. Growth Rates of Output and the Composition of Value Added Unit: Percent

	Growth rates of output			Composition of value added		
	Promoted	Non-promoted	Difference	Promoted	Non-promoted	Difference
1970	20.7	19.3	1.4	31.2	68.8	−37.7
1971	17.5	14.1	3.4	32.0	68.0	−36.1
1972	18.3	10.8	7.5	28.0	72.0	−44.1
1973	45.5	21.2	24.3	32.9	67.1	−34.2
1974	30.2	9.5	20.6	42.1	57.9	−15.8
1975	13.6	10.5	3.1	40.5	59.5	−19.0
1976	32.8	21.5	11.3	43.0	57.0	−13.9
1977	21.8	9.2	12.6	44.8	55.2	−10.3
1978	31.1	16.4	14.7	47.7	52.3	−4.5
1979	14.7	6.5	8.2	49.5	50.5	−1.1
1980	1.5	−1.8	3.3	48.5	51.5	−3.1
1981	16.4	4.3	12.1	50.2	49.8	0.4
1982	9.2	5.8	3.4	51.5	48.5	3.0
1983	22.9	10.5	12.3	52.8	47.2	5.7
1984	17.9	12.0	5.9	53.3	46.7	6.7
1985	7.6	6.8	0.7	53.8	46.2	7.6
1986	22.5	18.3	4.3	55.1	44.9	10.2
1987	23.8	16.0	7.7	55.2	44.8	10.5
1988	18.4	8.0	10.5	58.8	41.2	17.6
1989	8.1	1.0	7.0	59.3	40.7	18.6
1990	15.2	3.1	12.1	60.3	39.7	20.6
1991	11.9	6.6	5.3	60.6	39.4	21.1
1992	8.5	2.4	6.0	60.5	39.5	20.9
1993	9.8	−0.6	10.4	62.6	37.4	25.2
1994	12.5	6.6	6.0	64.0	36.0	28.1
1995	14.5	4.6	9.9	67.7	32.3	35.4
1996	9.7	0.6	9.1	67.8	32.2	35.6
1997	8.2	0.6	7.6	69.2	30.8	38.3
1998	−7.4	−9.4	2.0	70.1	29.9	40.2
1999	24.0	14.0	10.0	69.2	30.8	38.3
2000	19.1	7.4	11.8	70.4	29.6	40.7
2001	2.6	1.6	1.6	69.8	30.2	39.6
2002	10.0	7.7	5.3	70.1	29.9	40.2
2003	6.9	−1.7	10.8	71.9	28.1	43.9
2004	11.2	1.4	10.4	75.1	24.9	50.3
2005	9.5	3.2	7.7	75.6	24.4	51.2
2006	8.8	4.1	7.7	76.3	23.7	52.6
2007	9.6	4.4	6.5	77.5	22.5	55.1
2008	3.6	−1.3	6.5	78.9	21.1	57.8
2009	−0.9	−4.6	6.5	77.4	22.6	54.8

Source: Lee (2011)

Table 3. Growth of Value Added

	Manufacturing total	Heavy & Chemical	Light	Electric Machinery	Clothing & Footwear
A. Value-Added by Industry Groups				(billions of 1980 won, %)	
1966	1,192.5(100.0)	182.2(15.3)	844.4(70.8)	22.3	78.0
1970	2,554.1(100.0)	419.9(16.4)	1,627.4(63.7)	62.7	151.1
1973	4,432.0(100.0)	969.5(21.9)	2,753.1(62.1)	240.0	354.1
1975	5,744.1(100.0)	1,515.5(26.4)	3,419.8(59.5)	343.0	506.4
1978	9,925.4(100.0)	3,420.7(34.5)	5,299.4(53.4)	919.3	791.6
1980	10,903.6(100.0)	3,671.7(33.7)	5,867.5(53.8)	988.4	712.1
1983	13,752.5(100.0)	5,267.3(38.3)	7,074.1(51.4)	1,457.6	897.2
1985	16,401.4(100.0)	6,791.2(41.4)	8,038.0(49.0)	1,837.1	969.7
B. Average Annual Percentage Changes					
1966-70	21.0	23.2	17.8	29.5	18.0
1970-73	20.2	32.2	19.2	56.4	32.8
1973-75	13.8	25.0	11.5	19.5	19.6
1975-78	20.0	31.2	15.7	38.9	16.1
1978-80	4.8	3.6	5.2	3.7	-5.2
1980-83	8.0	12.8	6.4	13.8	8.0
1983-85	9.2	13.5	6.6	12.3	4.0
1970-78	18.5	30.0	15.9	39.9	23.0
1978-85	7.4	10.3	6.1	10.4	2.9

Source: Yoo (1990)

Two subgroups of manufacturing sector consisted of the heavy and chemistry group and the light industry group made a different path of growth in the same period. In table 3 it shows that growth of value added in HC increased more than 37 times, compared to the light industry that grew approximately 9.5 times in the 1966-85 period. For the average annual percentage changes, the HC industries grew almost two times faster than the Light industries (Yoo, 1990).

The Electric Machinery industry of HC group and the clothing and footwear industry in the Light group are similar in regards to they were both highly export-oriented and used the least capital intensive methods of production in each of groups. But the differences are that machinery was likely to be a more technology-intensive industry than clothing and footwear, and the former one was promoted by the state but the latter was not. As table 4 shows the Heavy &Chemical's capital intensity[2] were higher than Light industry, and Electric Machinery industry's capital intensity were higher than clothing & Footwear industry (Yoo, 1990).

Table 4. Capital Intensity

	Manufacturing total	Heavy & Chemical	Light	Electric Machinery	Clothing & Footwear
A. Capital Intensity				(Millions of 1980 won per worker)	
1966	3.9	6.9	3.1	2.3	0.3
1970	4.3	6.7	3.5	2.3	0.6
1973	5.9	8.2	4.8	2.4	0.8
1975	6.2	10.2	4.7	4.8	0.9
1978	7.4	12.5	5.3	4.5	1.4
1980	9.6	15.3	7.0	5.5	1.9
1983	11.1	16.0	8.3	6.7	2.6
1985	12.6	17.7	9.4	9.5	2.8
B. Average Annual Percentage Changes					
1966-70	2.5	-0.7	3.3	-0.3	14.4
1970-73	11.1	7.0	11.1	1.5	10.2
1973-75	2.8	11.9	-0.7	41.2	7.7
1975-78	5.7	7.1	4.2	-2.1	16.4
1978-80	14.1	10.3	14.9	10.0	14.0
1980-83	5.1	1.7	5.6	7.1	11.1
1983-85	6.3	5.1	6.4	19.0	4.4
1970-78	7.0	8.2	5.4	8.8	11.8
1978-85	7.9	5.0	8.4	11.2	10.0

Source: Yoo (1990)

However, the state's support was greater and longer than expected. In the debate Ha-Joon argues that pursuing industrial policy that aims to have a huge leap forward by defying from its comparative advantage is possible and the CAD strategy is encouraged although it is likely to be costly and long.

---

[2] Capital intensity refers to the capital-labor ratio, and employment growth and capital accumulation that affect the industries' capital intensities

However when state pursuing the CAD strategy should be cautious about the likely outcome of implementing an infant industry protection invented by industrial policy, which may deviate far from its latent comparative advantage.

Because as table 5 shows that industrial policy performance in Korea was not entirely successful, as seen that it failed to pay off until 1994 −cost of industrial policy outweighs its benefit, 'picked the winners' but at too high a cost (Lee, 2011). From the 1970s unit cost was increasing fast and large. Other studies by Korean economists found a similar result that there were considerable interim costs occurred to the heavy and chemical industry program in the 1970s and 80s, and the protection failed to satisfy the Mill Bastable Test[3] (Yoo, 1990).

This could be interpreted as the state pursued industrial policy too strongly (in other words, the state distorted the price mechanism 'got prices wrong' too severely and for too long), as it tried to develop prematurely promoted infant industries by attempting to increase its technology ladder or 'technological capabilities' at a pace that is beyond its accumulated learning experience and its latent comparative advantage.

As Lin (2011: 309) argues the CAD strategy can be very inefficient and costly, and the length of time pursuing this strategy depends on the government's resource mobilization and support. And one can argue that in case of Korea it was too long for the net benefit to pay off its costs. In other words, the industrial policy may have solved the 'static' problem of organization coordination, but it also did more harm than good in the long run because it impeded the functions of the natural-selection mechanism of the market economy (Burton, 1983).

---

[3] The test puts one of two conditions that require whether the protected industries are able to pay off the national losses during the protection period.

Table 5. Revised Net Effective Rate of Protection, Net Profitability and Unit Cost

	Revised Effective Rate of Protection			Net Profitability			Unit Cost		
	Promoted	Non-promoted	Difference	Promoted	Non-promoted	Difference	Promoted	Non-promoted	Difference
1970	0.088	−0.057	0.146	−0.162	−0.143	−0.019	1.265	1.078	0.187
1971				−0.302	−0.150	−0.152	1.422	1.072	0.350
1972				−0.229	−0.039	−0.190	1.347	0.958	0.390
1973				0.069	0.205	−0.136	1.025	0.723	0.301
1974				0.076	−0.041	0.117	1.021	0.934	0.087
1975	0.110	−0.117	0.228	−0.084	−0.063	−0.021	1.203	0.938	0.265
1976				−0.106	−0.014	−0.092	1.286	0.887	0.399
1977				−0.128	−0.052	−0.076	1.309	0.938	0.372
1978	0.255	−0.139	0.394	−0.132	0.037	−0.169	1.420	0.829	0.591
1979				−0.189	−0.052	−0.137	1.468	0.945	0.522
1980	0.216	−0.067	0.282	−0.523	−0.227	−0.296	1.852	1.145	0.706
1981				−0.409	−0.234	−0.175	1.659	1.157	0.502
1982				−0.326	−0.244	−0.082	1.491	1.173	0.318
1983	0.097	−0.055	0.152	−0.186	−0.117	−0.069	1.302	1.056	0.246
1984				−0.191	−0.165	−0.026	1.288	1.076	0.212
1985	0.064	−0.100	0.163	−0.180	−0.123	−0.057	1.255	1.011	0.244
1986				−0.108	−0.027	−0.081	1.192	0.914	0.278
1987				−0.132	−0.015	−0.117	1.237	0.888	0.349

	Revised Effective Rate of Protection			Net Profitability			Unit Cost		
	Promoted	Non-promoted	Difference	Promoted	Non-promoted	Difference	Promoted	Non-promoted	Difference
1988	0.101	−0.133	0.234	−0.097	−0.061	−0.036	1.208	0.920	0.288
1989				−0.208	−0.138	−0.070	1.321	1.009	0.312
1990	0.086	−0.094	0.180	−0.186	−0.135	−0.051	1.287	1.028	0.259
1991				−0.227	−0.183	−0.044	1.308	1.091	0.217
1992				−0.213	−0.179	−0.034	1.262	1.114	0.149
1993	0.028	−0.044	0.072	−0.161	−0.177	0.016	1.193	1.125	0.069
1994				−0.120	−0.157	0.037	1.147	1.113	0.034
1995	0.020	−0.031	0.051	−0.068	−0.181	0.113	1.089	1.144	−0.055
1996				−0.199	−0.229	0.030			
1997				−0.269	−0.243	−0.026			
1998				−0.439	−0.422	−0.017			
1999				−0.218	−0.278	0.060			
2000				−0.259	−0.196	−0.063			
2001				−0.304	−0.138	−0.166			
2002				0.020	−0.037	0.057			
2003				0.038	−0.070	0.108			
2004				0.220	−0.033	0.253			
2005				0.142	0.042	0.101			
2006				0.081	0.040	0.040			
2007				0.057	−0.032	0.089			
2008				−0.126	−0.101	−0.025			
2009				0.019	0.001	0.018			

Source: Lee (2011)

8. Conclusion

Lin's New Structural Economics and growth identification and facilitation framework (GIFF) model by Lin and Monga reinvigorated the debate on an appropriate role of growth policy, state's industrial policy in development economics. Few would doubt about the importance of structural change, the basic economic principle of trade theory, and the development of industries in consistent with latent comparative advantage. But the discussion or industrial policy debate has not been closed yet but has been remained a topical issue. The focus of the question should be a disagreement of capacity of developing countries - how is the ability of the state to implement it and to what degree countries should follow strategically industrialization consistent of their static comparative advantages.

This paper discussed theoretical arguments of comparative advantage in industrial policy in Korea, based on the recent debate between Justin Lin and Ha-Joon Chang. The debate prevailed both agreement and disagreement on the issue, as similarities they agreed on the view of an importance of the role of state in industrial upgrading (which is a big step forward from the conventional wisdom of neoclassical economic approach and the World Bank's previous policy descriptions), the basic economic principle of comparative advantage theory. However, how far a country's industrial policy is allowed to deviate from its comparative advantage is still not clear. But at least this paper suggests in contrast to Lin's argument of CAF strategy, the positive intersectoral externalities between the low skilled labor intensive and high-tech, skilled capital intensive industries do not entirely hold as given an example of steel industry, and it is noticed that Korea deviated too far from its latent comparative advantage and the costs were high and the duration time was long even though the most of the state's plans and policy was somehow successful to bring fruitful results in the end.

Therefore, this fact also discredits the Ha-Joon's long period of infant industry argument - a state should protect the promoted industries as long as they become mature enough to compete in international market.

This paper suggests a new adjusted approach taking two sides' arguments that the temporary appropriate state intervention in prompting industrial upgrading, and the comparative advantage facilitating (CAF) strategy would be important but also the comparative advantage defying (CAD) strategy, in other words creating comparative advantage through increasing technological capabilities –technology acquisition, skilled labor force, human capital development, etc., would be needed to move the ladder of industrial upgrading from the low to the high end industrial sectors - where in the linkage between the former and the latter in the domestic value chain would not be strong except few. Moreover, as the experience of Korea shows in the process of industrial upgrading, the role of state was crucial. Although not all of its policies were conducive to economic growth and industrialization, and it is still debatable how much credits for the success to be contributed to the state. But, its outward oriented, public and private integrated approach, international benchmarking to industrial policy as well as its learning by doing process interlinked with bank and selected firms were quite important to maximize the benefits of industrialization with limited resources.

However, it is a grand question that not only how can a country recognize industries with its latent comparative advantage and facilitate it, but also how much can a country defy its comparative advantage to create its competitive advantage without having a great distortion of resource allocation by market function. This would be conditional upon variable factors such as a country's political, economic, social conditions, cultural idiosyncrasies, factor endowments, and changes in world market. And the question of replicability of Korea (and East Asia's success) has been persistent theme in the debate, thereby, the generalization should be avoided. This issue is beyond the scope of this research paper, so it would require for further research for a correct understanding of the past experiences, however, the unique case of Korean industrial policy would provide some valuable lessons of critical importance for other countries.

9. Bibliography

Aghion, P, Boulanger, J, & Cohen, E, 2011, 'Rethinking industrial policy. Bruegel Policy Brief 2011/04, June 2011', Archive of European Integration, EBSCO*host*, viewed 27 March 2013.

Amsden, H, Alice 1989, *Asia's Next Giant: South Korea and Late Industrialization, Oxford.*
--------------   2001 - The Rise of "The Rest" [Elektronisk resurs] Challenges to the West From Late-Industrializing Economies.

Akamatsu, Kaname,1962, 'A Historical Pattern of Economic Growth in Developing Countries', The Developing Economies, Preliminary Issue No.1: 3–25.

Bryman, Alan, 2008, *Social research methods.* 4th edition, Oxford: Oxford University Press.

Burton, J, 1983, Picking Losers...? The Political Economy of Industrial Policy. London: Institute of Economic Affairs.

Chang, Ha-Joon, 2003, Rethinking Development Economics,
---------------------2002 Kicking Away the Ladder – Development Strategy in Historical Perspective, London: Anthem Press, ch. 2.
---------------------1995 Role of state in economic change, Oxford University Press.
---------------------1994 The Political Economy of Industrial Policy, The Macmillan Press LTD.

Chang, H-J and Grabel Ilene, 2004, Reclaiming Development –An Alternative Economic Policy Manual. Zed Books.

Chen Shiyi, Jefferson Gary H, and Zhang Jun, 2011, Structural Change, Productivity Growth, and Structural Transformation in China. China Economic Review 22.

Gerschenkron, A., 1962, *Economic Backwardness in Historical Perspective:A Book of Essays.* Cambridge, MA: Belknap Press of Harvard University Press.

Greenwald, B., and J.E. Stiglitz. ,2006, "Helping Infant Economies Grow: Foundations of Trade Policies for Developing Countries." American Economic Review: AEA Papers and Proceedings 96(2): 141–6.

Hausmann, R. and Rodrik, D.,2003, 'Economic Development as Self-Discovery', Journal of Development Economics 72 (December).

Hawtry, R.G, 1937, Capital and Employment. London: Longmans.

Il Sakong and Koh Youngsun ,2010, The Korean Economy: Six decades of Growth and

Development. KDI

Ju, J., Lin, J. Y. and Wang, Y., 2009, Endowment Structures, Industrial Dynamics and Economic Growth. Policy Research Working Paper No. 5055. Washington, DC: World Bank.

Kim C.Y.,2011, *From Despair to Hope: Economic Policymaking in Korea, 1945–1979*. Seoul: Korea Development Institute.

Kim, C, & Hong, M, 2010, 'Education Policy and Industrial Development: The Cases of Korea and Mexico', *Journal Of International And Area Studies*, 17, 2, pp. 21-30, EconLit, EBSCOhost, viewed 8 May 2013.

Krueger A.O. 1974. The political economy of the rent-seeking society. *American Economic Review*, **64** (3), 291–303.

Krugman, P. & Obsfeld, M. (2006) *International Economics: Theory and Policy*, 7th ed. (Boston: Pearson).

Kuznets, S. 1966, Modern Economic Growth. New Haven, CT: Yale University Press.

Lee, J, 2011, 'The Performance of Industrial Policy: Evidence from Korea', *International Economic Journal*, 25, 1, pp. 1-27, Business Source Complete, EBSCOhost, viewed 2 May 2013.

Lee, J, Clacher, I, & Keasey, K, 2012, 'Industrial Policy as an Engine of Economic Growth: A Framework of Analysis and Evidence from South Korea (1960-96)', *Business History*, 54, 5, pp. 713-740, EconLit, EBSCOhost, viewed 27 March 2013.

Lieberman, M, & Kang, J, 2008, 'How to measure company productivity using value-added: A focus on Pohang Steel (POSCO)', *Asia Pacific Journal Of Management*, 25, 2, pp. 209-224, Business Source Complete, EBSCOhost, viewed 3 May 2013.

Lim, W, 2012, 'Chaebol and Industrial Policy in Korea', *Asian Economic Policy Review*, 7, 1, pp. 69-86, EconLit, EBSCOhost, viewed 8 May 2013.
----------2011, 'Joint Discovery and Upgrading of Comparative Advantage: Lessons from Korea's Development Experience' in Shahrokh Fardoust, Yongbeom Kim and Claudia Sepulveda (eds.), *Postcrisis Growth and Development: A Development Agenda for the G-20*. Washington, DC: World Bank.

Lin, Justin Yifu, 2011, New Structural Economics – A Framework for Rethinking development and policy
------------------- 2011, "From Flying Geese to Leading Dragons: New Opportunities and Strategies for Structural Transformation in Developing Countries." WIDER Annual Lecture 15, Helsinki: UNU-WIDER. (A shorter version of this paper is forthcoming in Global Policy.)

------------------,2009, Economic Development and Transition: Thought, Strategy and Viability. Cambridge: Cambridge University Press.

Lin, J-Y and Chang H-J, 2009, "Should Industrial Policy in Developing Countries Conform to Comparative Advantage or Defy It? A Debate Between Justin Lin and Ha-Joon Chang," *Development Policy Review*, 27 (5).

Lin J.Y. & Monga C. ,2010. Growth identification and facilitation: The role of the state in the dynamics of structural change. Policy Research Working Paper no. 5313.Washington, DC: The World Bank.

Mao, R, & Yao, Y 2012, 'Structural Change in a Small Open Economy: An Application to South Korea', *Pacific Economic Review*, 17, 1, pp. 29-56, EconLit, EBSCO*host*, viewed 24 May 2013

Mussa, Michael ,1978, 'Dynamic Adjustment in the Heckscher-Ohlin-Samuelson Model', Journal of Political Economy 86 (5): 775–91.

Murphy, Kevin M., Andrei Shleifer, and Robert W. Vishny. 1989a. "Income Distribution, Market Size, and Industrialization." *Quarterly Journal of Economics* 104 (August): 537–64.
–––. 1989b. "Industrialization and Big Push." *Journal of Political Economy* 97 (October): 1003–26.

North Douglass C,1993, The New Institutional Economics and Development, An essay from American Economic Society Meeting in January 1992

Pack, Howard and Saggi, Kamal,2006, 'Is There a Case for Industrial Policy? A Critical Survey', *World Bank Research Observer,* Fall.

Reddy, Sanjay, and Camelia Minoiu, 2009, "Real Income Stagnation of Countries 1960–2001." Journal of Development Studies 45 (1): 1–23.

Sato, H, 2009, 'The East Asian Development Experience: The Miracle, the Crisis and the Future - by Ha-Joon Chang', *Developing Economies*, 47, 2, p. 226, Publisher Provided Full Text Searching File, EBSCO*host*, viewed 8 May 2013.

Saure, Philip, 2007, 'Revisiting the Infant Industry Argument', Journal of Development Economics 84 (1): 104–17.

Shin, Jang-Sup and Chang, H-J, 2003, Restructuring Korean Inc. Routledge

Singh, A 2011, 'Comparative Advantage, Industrial Policy and the World Bank: Back to First Principles', *Policy Studies*, 32, 4, pp. 447-460, EconLit, EBSCO*host*, viewed 31 March 2013

Singh, A.,1998, Competitive markets and economic development. In: P. Arestis and M. Sawyer, eds. Political economy of economic policy. London: Macmillan, 60106.

Solow, Robert M,1957, "Technical Change and the Aggregate Production Function." Review of Economics and Statistics 39(3): 312–20.

Suehiro, Akira, 2008, Catch-up Industrialization – The Trajectory and Prospect of East Asian Economies. Translated by Tom Gill, University of Hawaii Press.

Stiglitz, Joseph E, 2011, Rethinking Development Economics, The World Bank Research Observer, The Oxford University Press on the behalf of the World Bank Group.

Succar, Patricia, 1987, "The Need for Industrial Policy in LDCs – A Restatement of the Infant-Industry Argument." *International Economic Review* 28: 521-534.

Todd Buchholz, 2007, New Ideas from Dead Economists: An Introduction to Modern Economic Thought. New York: Plume Books.

Yoo, Jung-Ho, 1996, Challenges to the Newly Industrialized Countries: A reinterpretation of Korea's Growth Experience. Korea Development Institute
---------------, 1990, The Industrial Policy of the 1970s and the Evolution of the Manufacturing Sector in Korea, Korea development institute

Wade, R., 1990, Governing the market: economic theory and the role of government in East Asian industrialization. Princeton, NJ: Princeton University Press.

World Bank, 1993, The East Asian miracle. New York: Oxford University Press.

Printed in Great Britain
by Amazon